CITY-GATES
QUEENS, N.Y.
718 939•9700

I0485149

A Mark Dahle Portfolio

Mama
Yah's
Kitchen

Mark Dahle Portfolios can be read in a few minutes and enjoyed for a lifetime. Unlike many picture books, the text is not related to the art. This might seem a little weird at first. One thing that helps is to order more portfolios until you get used to it. Until then, feel free to draw your own pictures of Mama Yah's restaurant on the pages if you like.

This portfolio includes twenty-five beautiful industrial photographs from Manhattan, a photo of a brilliant 2 x 3 foot painting (at the right), and a story about a busload of hungry passengers on a trip to the best restaurant in the world.

Photographs in this book are available in limited editions. See http://www.MarkDahle.com for more information and for previews of upcoming portfolios.

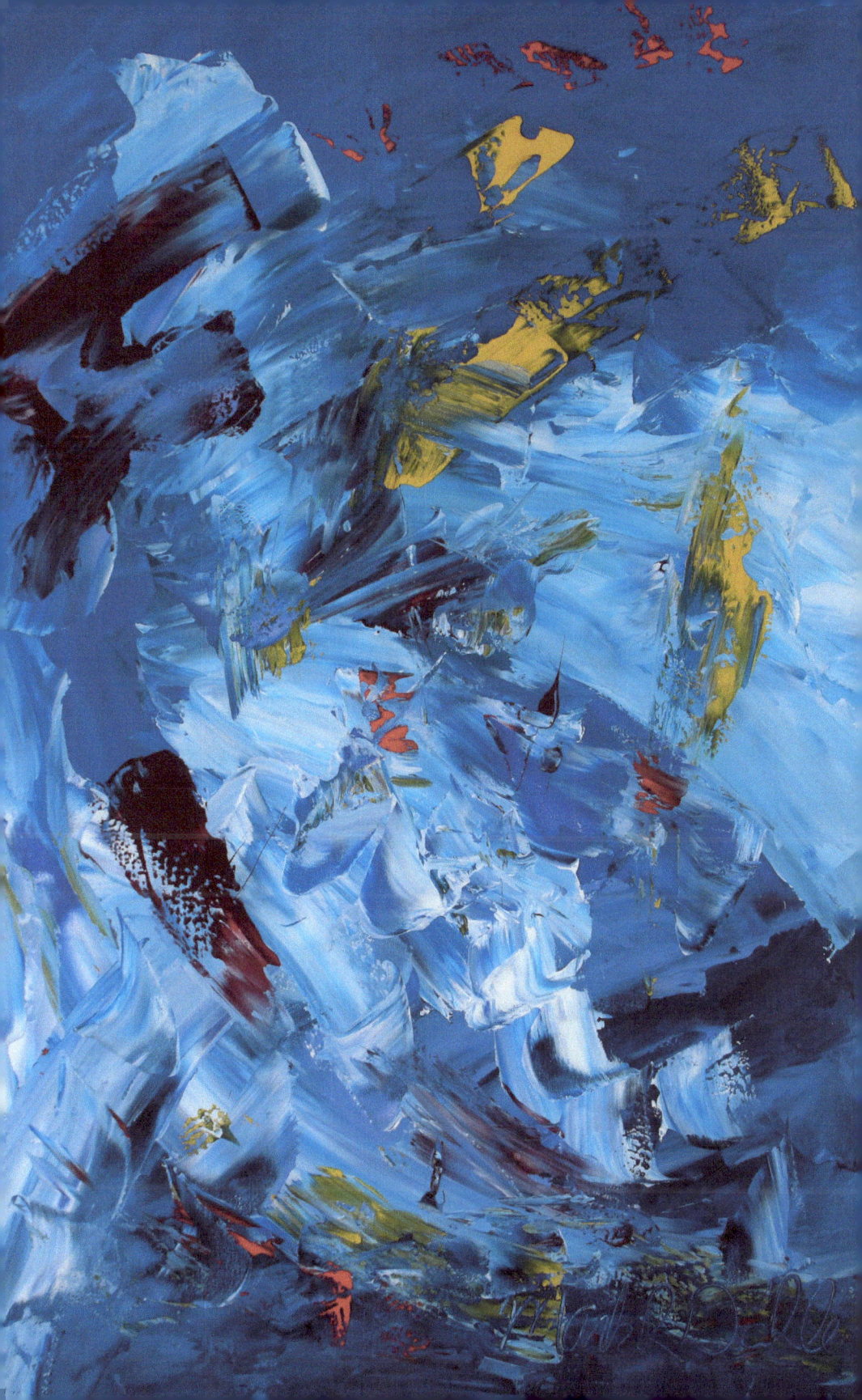

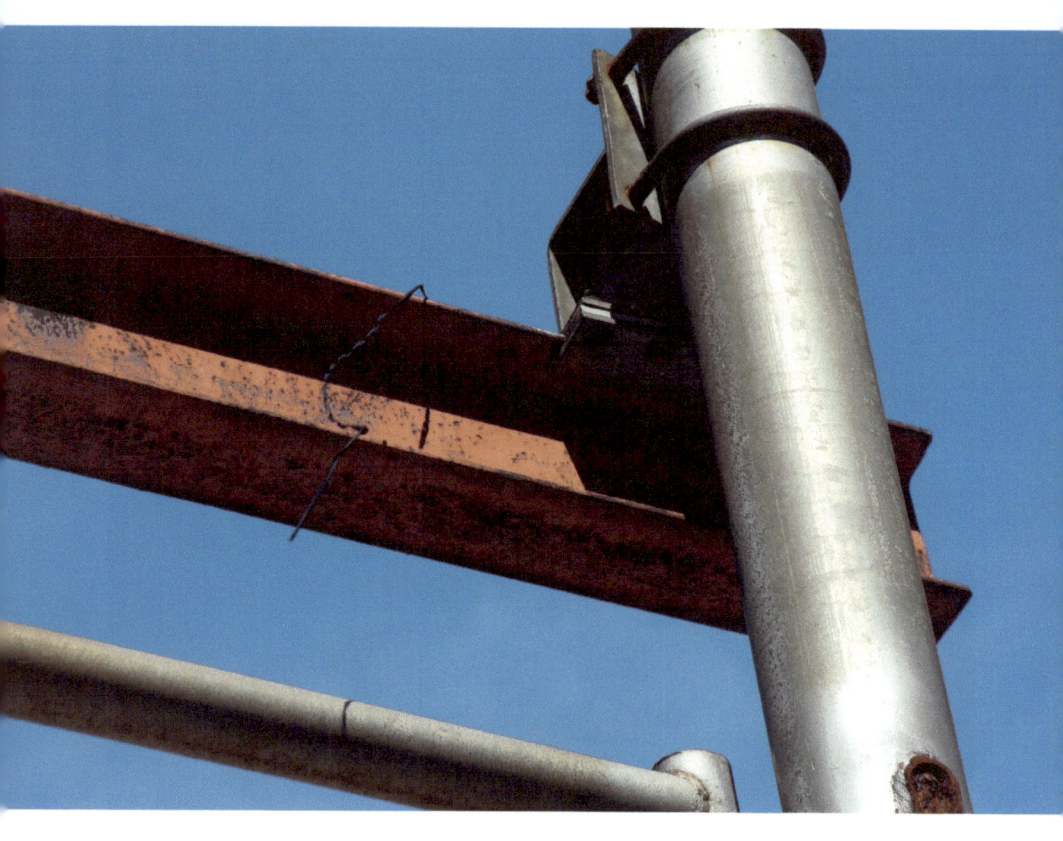

4

Mama Yah produced, with several ghost writers, the world's most famous cookbook. She had created it partly because her restaurant was so far out of the way. She thought having a cookbook would allow people to taste her recipes before they made the trek all the way out to her restaurant, a sampler before they got to the real thing.

Surprisingly, even though her cookbook was a *huge* seller, very few people actually opened it, read a recipe, and followed the instructions. Mostly people just owned copies and kept them out for display. People read from the cookbook like they would read a fantasy novel, imagining how good the creations might be without ever going to the bother of following the directions and tasting things for themselves.

Partly because of the popularity of her cookbook, Mama Yah's restaurant was famous throughout the world. Often it was described in hushed tones. Some people had even heard that if you ever got to eat in her kitchen, you'd never want to eat anywhere else. The food was said to be that good.

Because of the cookbook's fame and
the fame of the restaurant, busloads of
adventurers signed up to travel long distances
to sample Mama Yah's cooking. This is the
story of one of those trips.

~

Early one morning about 40 passengers
eagerly boarded Matt's bus. Some had not
eaten breakfast so they'd be especially
hungry when they arrived at Mama Yah's.

Most of those passengers hadn't counted on
how *long* a trip it was.

A couple hours into the journey, Jamil stood
up and addressed the other passengers.

"Let's not wait," he said. "Let's stop on the
way for a little bite – something just to tide us
over."

Saura, sitting next to him, didn't usually
speak up, but the audacity of his suggestion

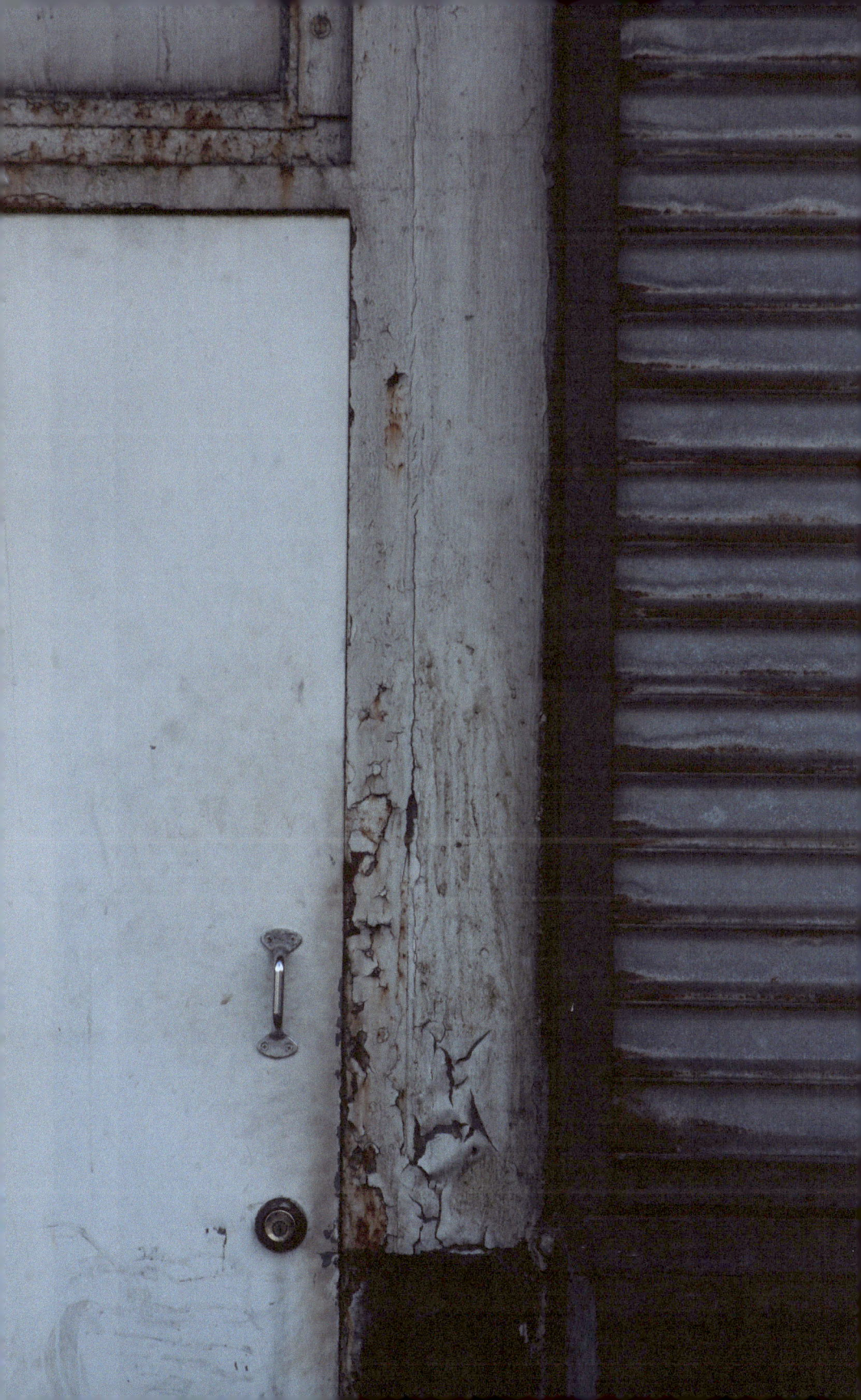

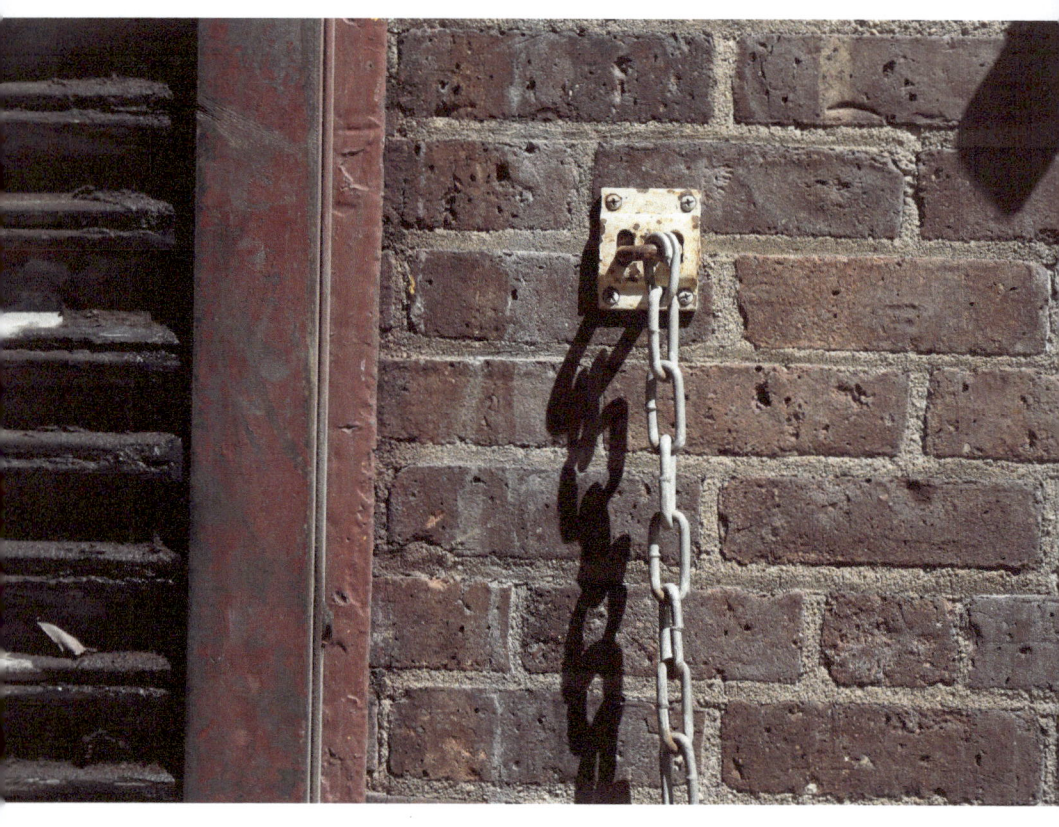

shocked her into responding. "You've *got* to be kidding!" she exclaimed. "This is a tour to Mama Yah's Kitchen. We're *not* going to stop partway there and get something half rate!"

Ruby and Don also said they thought everyone should wait and save their appetites. Saura was relieved at how the discussion was going. But she didn't know how hungry some of the other passengers were. And she hadn't counted on Matt, the bus driver.

Matt said they still had a *long* way to travel, and he knew the perfect place where they could stop for a bite. They could get as much or as little as each person wanted – they could even stay on the bus and wait for everyone else to come back, if they chose.

To the relief of Jamil and some of the most desperate passengers, a chorus of voices urged Matt to stop when he came to this spot.

It wasn't long before an enormous sign could be seen, far in the distance. If you were hungry, the sign was especially beautiful. Its brilliantly colored neon and flashing lights blinked on and off with a simple message: "EAT!"

A flashing arrow pointed to the entrance. The sign blinked on and off. "EAT! EAT! EAT!"

The sign convinced several holdouts that stopping part way was the best plan, and even Ruby and Don decided to go in when they saw how exciting everything looked.

When Matt finally pulled in to the enormous parking lot, some of the holdouts were encouraged by something else. The parking lot was *full* of buses and cars.

"If there are this many people here," said Kala, "this is *bound* to be a great place to eat. Maybe as great as Mama Yah's Kitchen."

"Maybe greater," said Jaslene.

"Maybe," said Aki, "this restaurant is about to become famous and we'll have discovered it

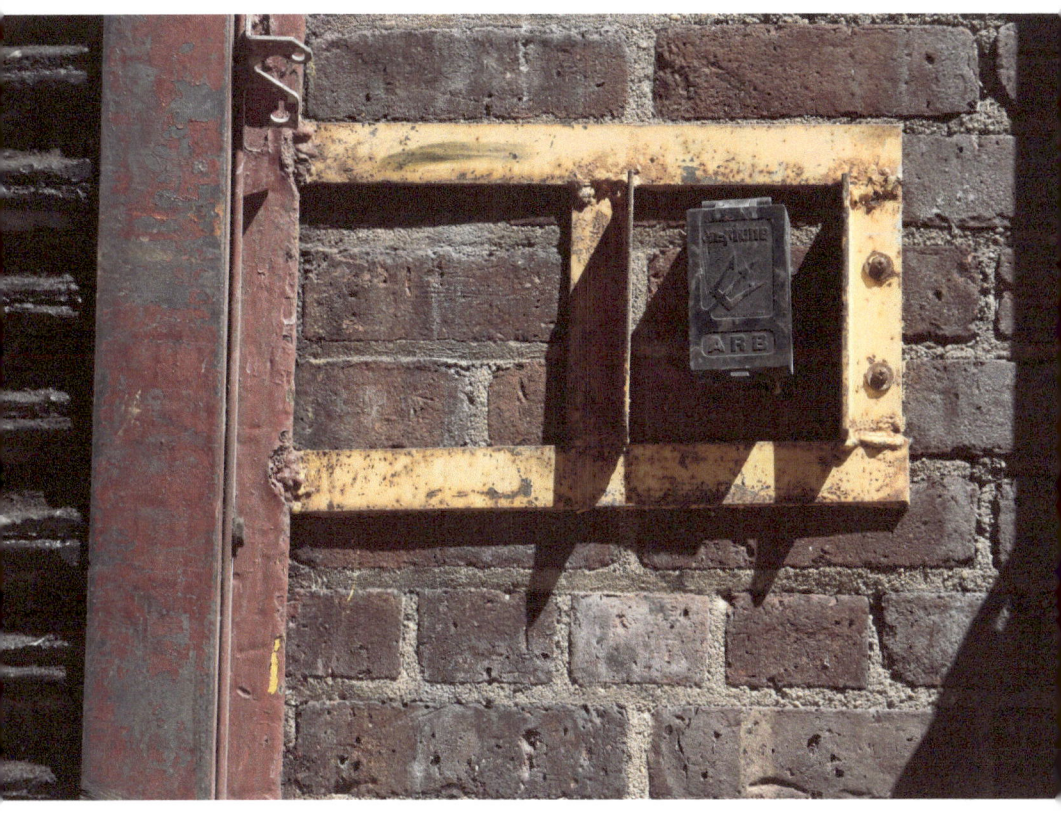

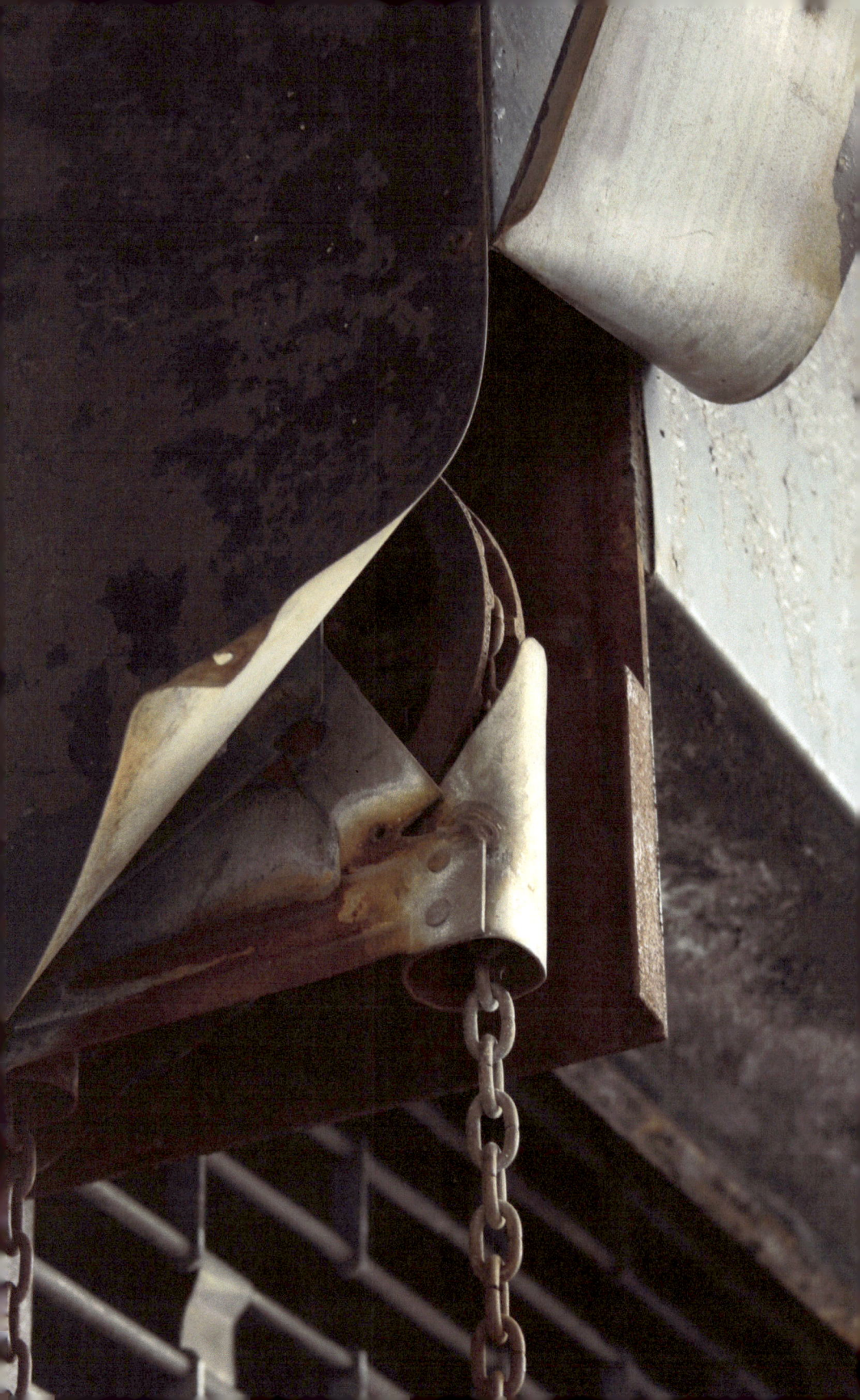

early. We'll be able to say we ate here before most people heard about it!"

What they didn't know (Matt didn't tell them) was that Matt and the other bus drivers got a percentage of sales whenever they dropped off tour groups. As a result, *lots* of buses stopped. The cars were all there because people figured with all the buses parked out front, the restaurant *must* be great.

Most of the passengers got off Matt's bus, their mouths watering for an appetizer that would tide them over until they got to Mama Yah's. A few who hadn't decided whether to leave or not were convinced by how many others left. But eight passengers stayed on board, determined to save their appetites. Matt, thinking about his percentage of sales, tried to persuade them that it was a *long* way to Mama Yah's and they'd never make it without a small bite. He convinced Jim, Liu and Wen to leave, all of whom regretted it later. But Saura and four others stayed on the bus, waiting.

Jack was one of the five who stayed behind. He was crippled, and it hurt whenever he moved. When he had boarded the bus, the only space available for him was all the way in the back. He *might* have gotten off the bus, but it hurt so much to move and it would have taken so much effort that he told himself he'd wait and save his strength for later.

No one leaving the bus offered to bring Jack anything when they returned, and the other four passengers who stayed behind were all talking excitedly together, up towards the front. The four weren't *trying* to exclude Jack, they just didn't think about going to the back of the bus to be with him. Jack was hungry, tired, cold, and somewhat lonely. He passed the time by thinking about Mama Yah.

Everyone who *hadn't* stayed on the bus rushed into the building and was surprised. This was not *one* restaurant. This was a *collection* of restaurants. The passengers were ecstatic. Look at all their choices!

The dozen or so restaurants were built in an

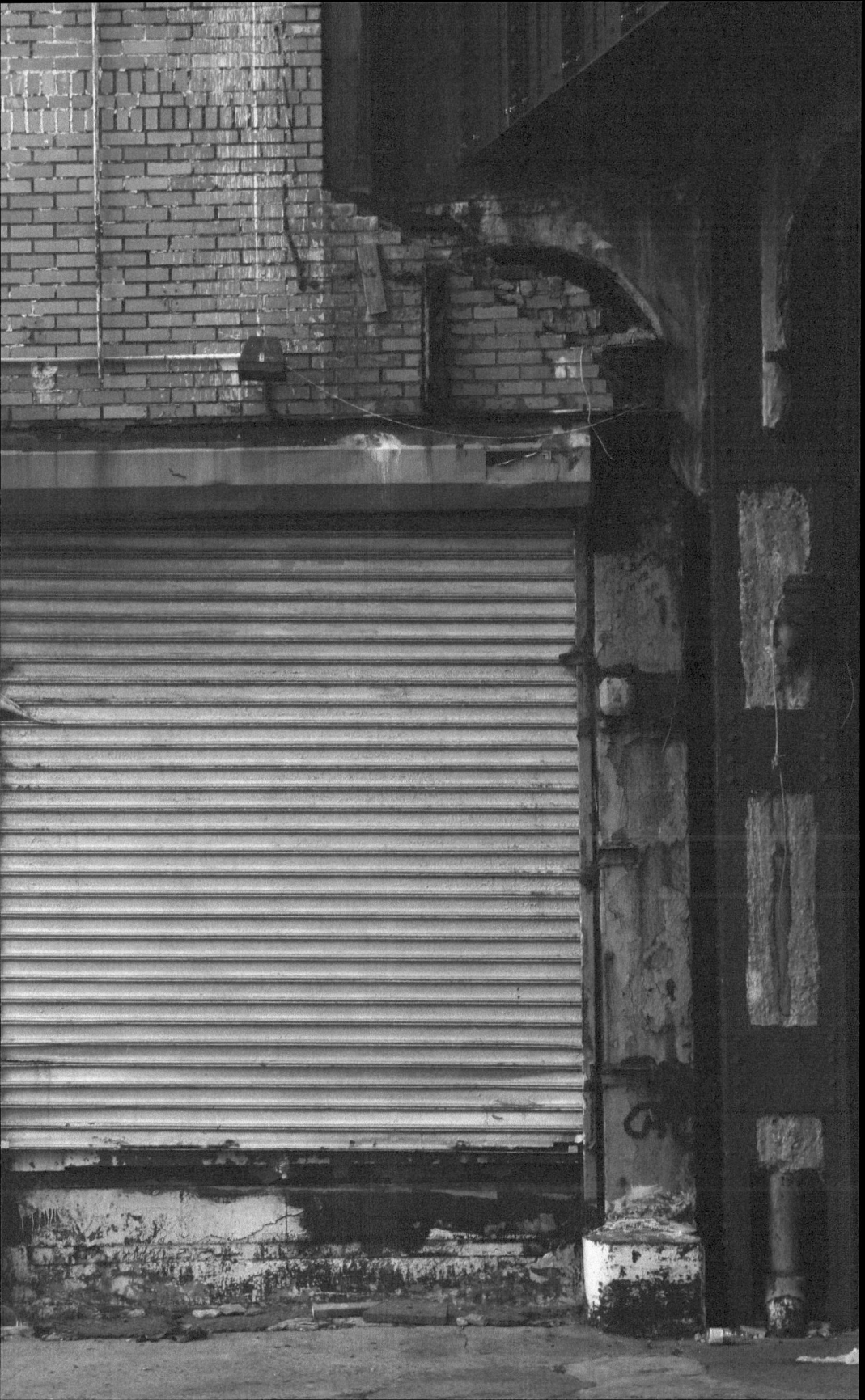

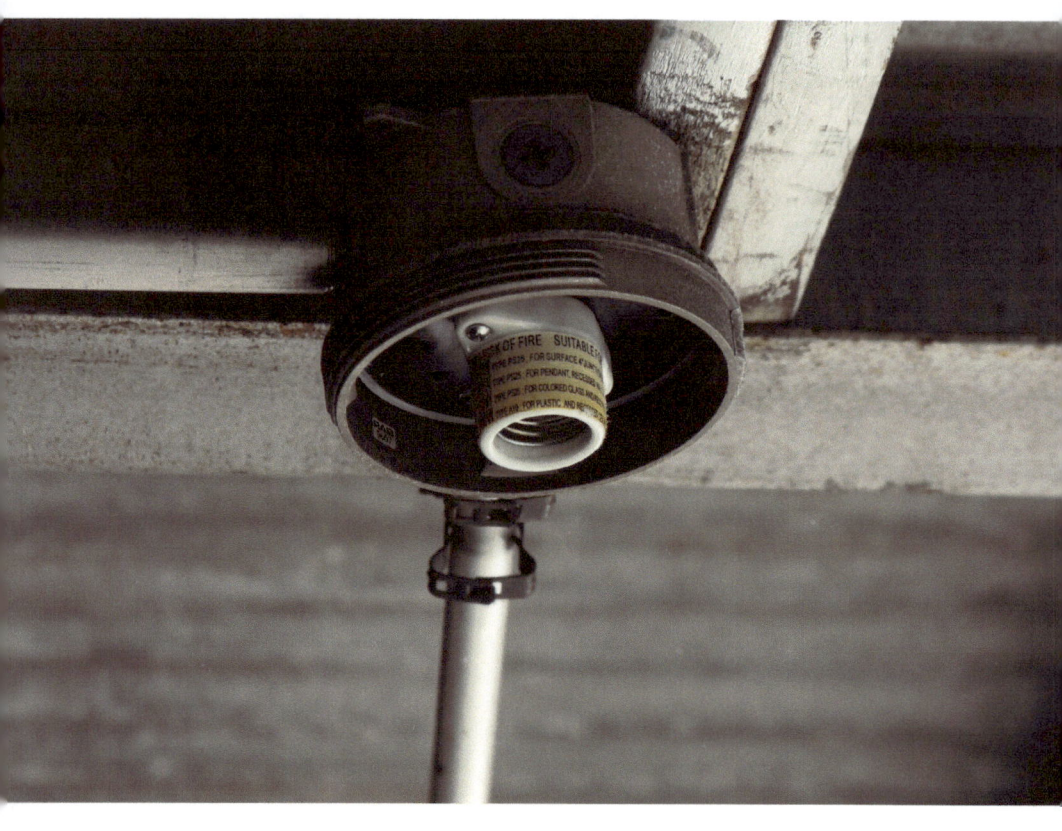

attractive circle around a large central eating area. You might be picturing a food court at a mall when I describe it this way. But that is *not* the image you should have! These were *great* looking restaurants. No offense to the chains at the malls you've been to, but if you saw the difference, you'd have no trouble figuring out where you'd like to eat! This was a dazzlingly beautiful collection of restaurants with hundreds of different menu items, all encircling a central court with a spectacular fountain.

Caleb and Ryan and Isabel hurried into the first restaurant because they saw something unexpected in the window: A sign announced that this restaurant used Mama Yah's cookbook!

"We'll be able to taste Mama Yah's cooking before we get to her restaurant," said Isabel.

"This may be good enough that we won't have to go the whole way!" said Caleb.

A couple others from the bus followed them

inside, while many chose other restaurants in the circle.

The cooks in the first restaurant actually *did* use Mama Yah's Cookbook as advertised. What they did not advertise was the particular *way* they used her cookbook. The cooks would flip open the recipe book, read one line, and then flip to another section to read a second line. From one recipe the cook might read, "Peel ten carrots." From another page: "Shred 10 onions." From another: "Add one gallon of molasses." From another: "Broil at 500 degrees." From another: "Cook one hour." They'd get the title of their creation from a final page, like "Egg Custard Delight."

The result was that their version of Egg Custard Delight varied rather wildly from the version served in Mama Yah's Kitchen and looked nothing like the picture of it in her cookbook.

The only thing really standard in this particular restaurant was that they promoted and sold Mama Yah's Cookbook, which many people

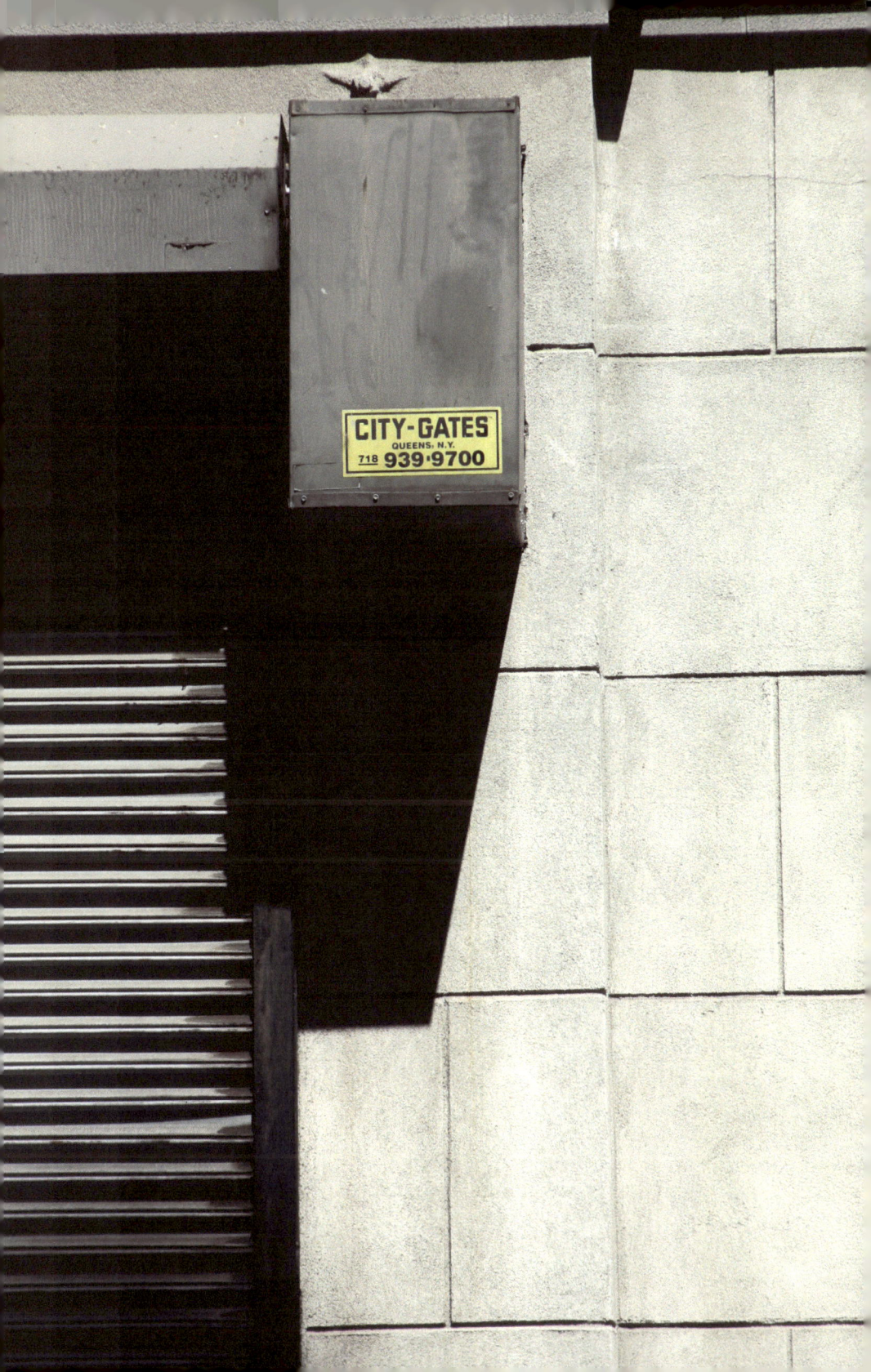

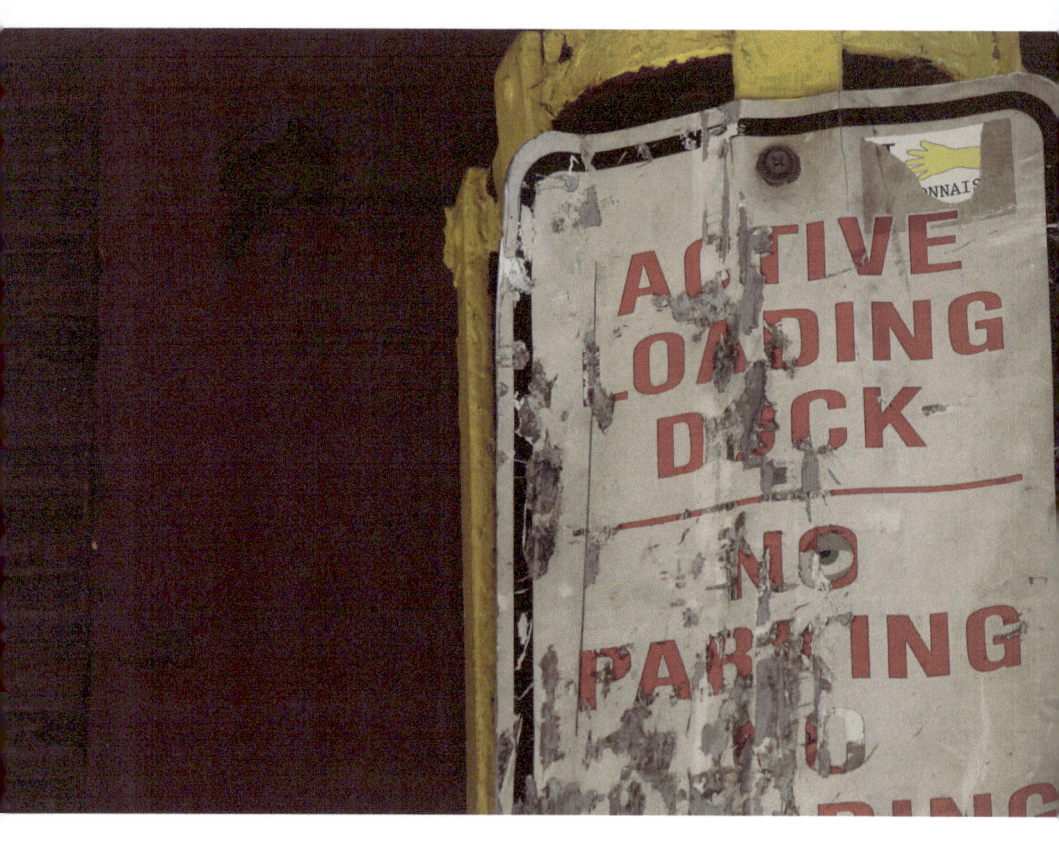

bought if they hadn't ordered the Egg Custard Delight.

When the passengers from Matt's bus entered the restaurant, they didn't know any of this. Ryan, unfortunately, *loved* Egg Custard Delight. He nearly bought a round for the entire table. In the end, they decided to each sample a different dessert and share. When the group saw the Egg Custard Delight, however, only Isabel decided to try some with Ryan. They were both sorry later.

~

Each of the other passengers had a slightly different story when they got back on the bus an hour and a half later.

Helen had decided, with so many good-looking restaurants, to try something different at each so she could say she had eaten at all of them. But by the time she got to restaurant number eleven, she was not feeling hungry and ordered to go boxes at the last two only out of principle.

Liu decided to try the *same* menu item at each restaurant to see how they compared. He started with the last restaurant and worked backwards, which was very lucky because he chose to compare their Egg Custard Delights. He got around half the circle before deciding the experiment wasn't worth it.

When the passengers later compared notes, they found that although they had each intended to eat "just a tiny bite," only one person had managed to do that, and he did it by not eating *anything*.

Javier had gotten off the bus, intending to eat a big meal. But when he saw all the great looking restaurants, he changed his mind and decided to wait for Mama Yah's Kitchen. He figured if these restaurants looked this good, Mama Yah's must be spectacular.

Everyone else who had gotten off the bus found that they had eaten more than they intended. Some had eaten *much* more.

Helen, Andy and Floyd weren't done eating

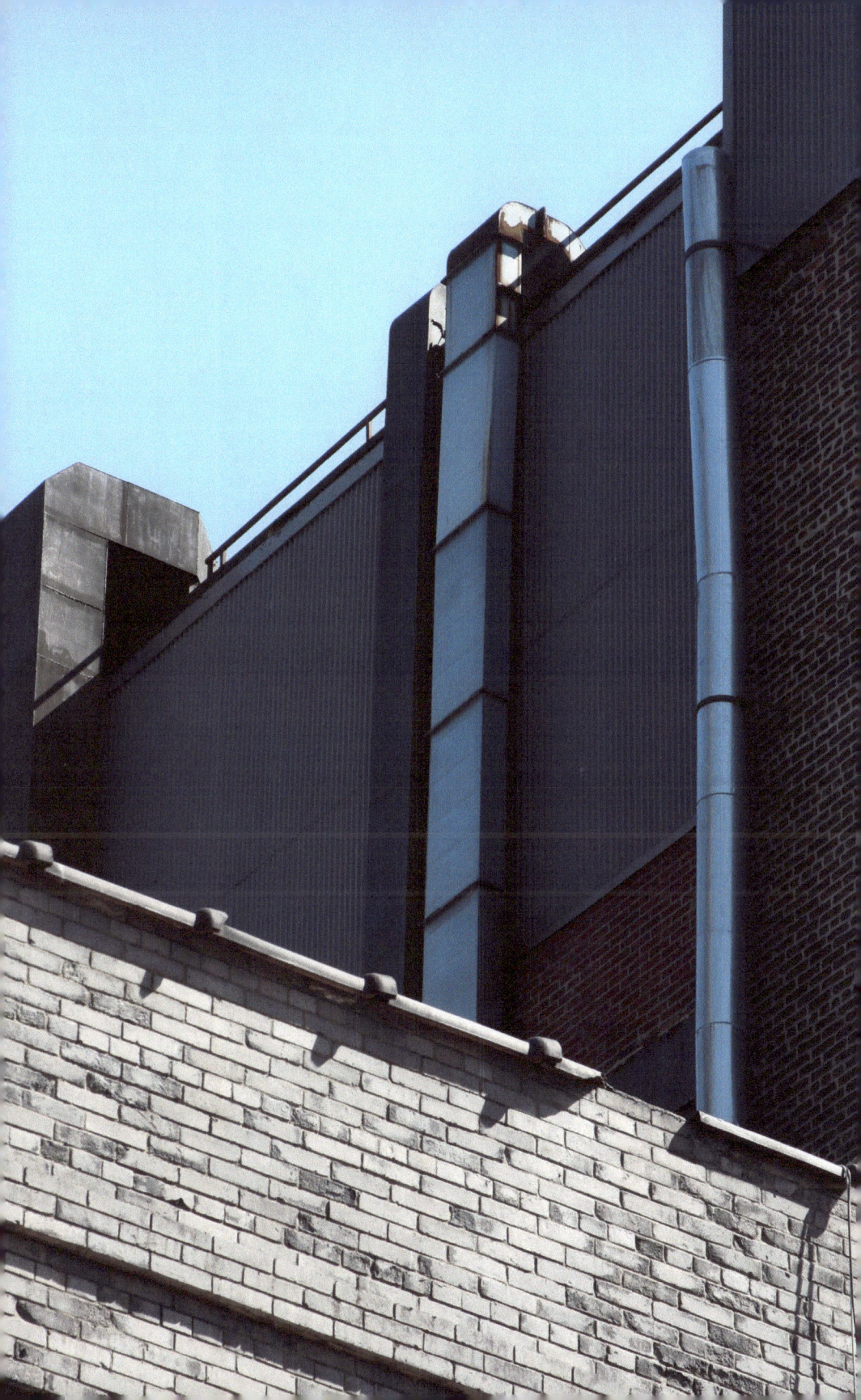

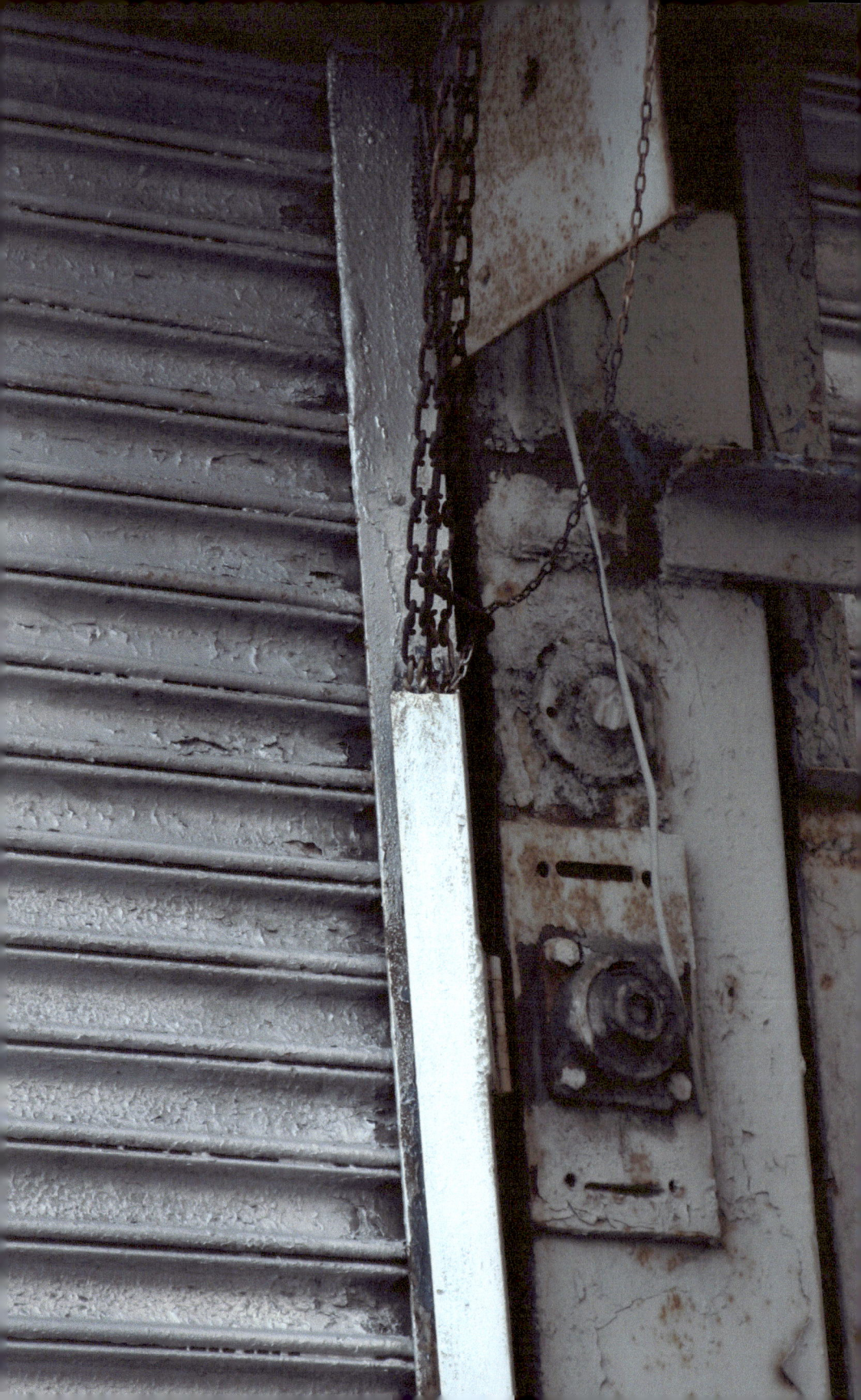

when their time was up, so they brought their leftovers onto the bus. They offered to give samples to Javier and the four people up front who had remained behind. They each wanted the people who sampled their leftovers to say that what *they* had brought back was the best, and several fights broke out on this account.

To try to avoid getting caught in the fights, Javier broke down and tried something from each of them – and then, to avoid hurting their feelings, had seconds.

Ruby and Aki also brought leftovers when they got back on the bus. But they were convinced that *their* leftovers were the best, and they refused to share or trade with anyone. They wanted to keep the best for themselves. Several more fights broke out because of that.

When all was said and done, Matt was about the only person who was happy they had stopped.

As luck would have it, Jack got the worst of it.

He was caught in several of the fights, since he was unable to move out of the way very quickly. Afterwards, everyone said Jack was not injured on purpose. But he *was* injured several times by blows intended for others. To be completely truthful, however, it must be said that some of the passengers were so worked up they didn't care *who* they hit, just as long as they hit *someone.*

Shortly after this, the bus turned off the main highway onto a narrow dirt road through the countryside that led to Mama Yah's Kitchen. If you've traveled in a bus on a dirt road, you can probably guess that some bumping was involved at this point in their trip. With all the bad cooking and overeating and stress and exhaustion from fighting and the bumping – not to mention the injuries – it wasn't long before a couple of the passengers were *very* ill, and nobody was feeling great.

During this stage of the journey, several of the passengers said they had had enough, and they demanded that the whole busload turn around and go home.

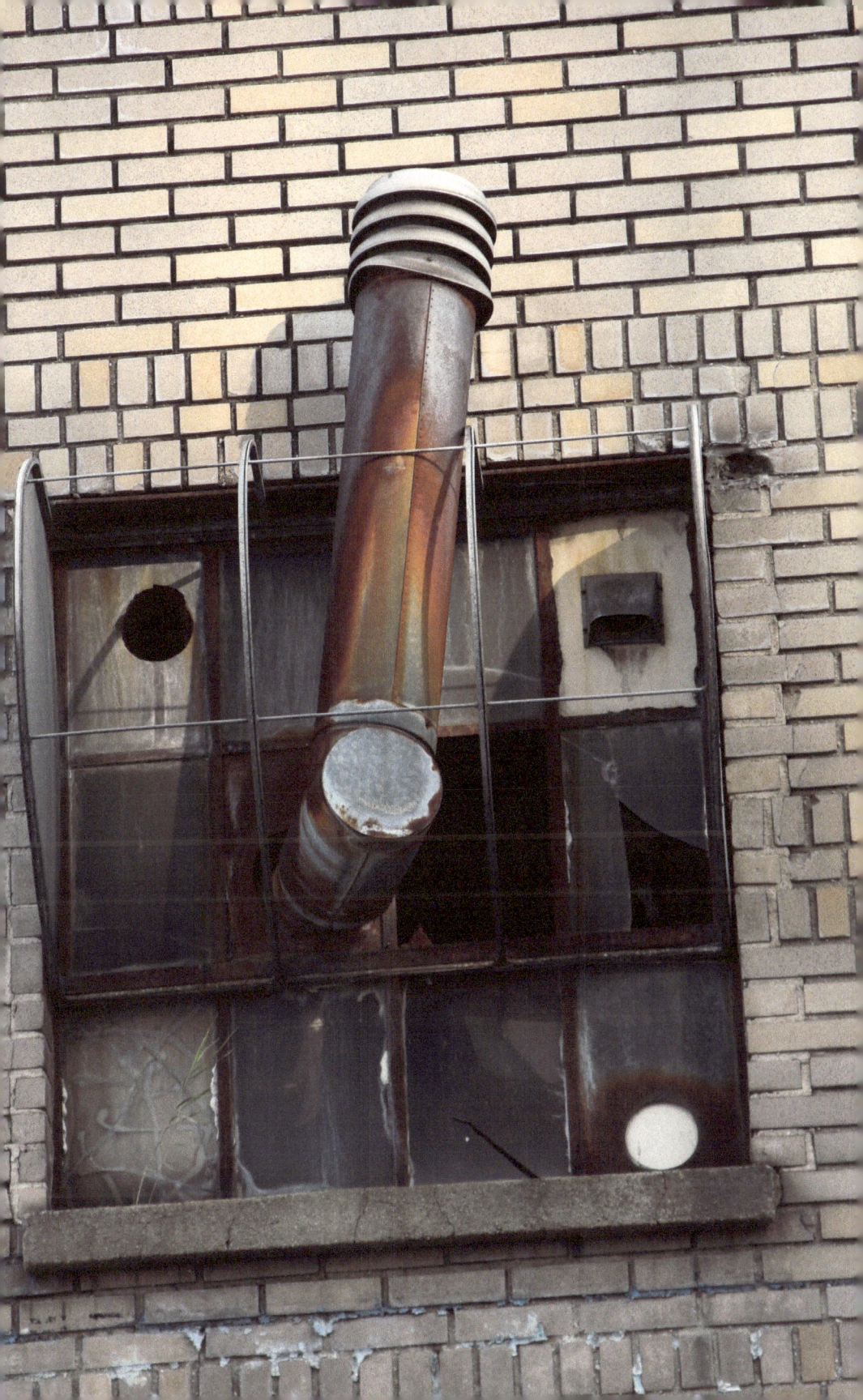

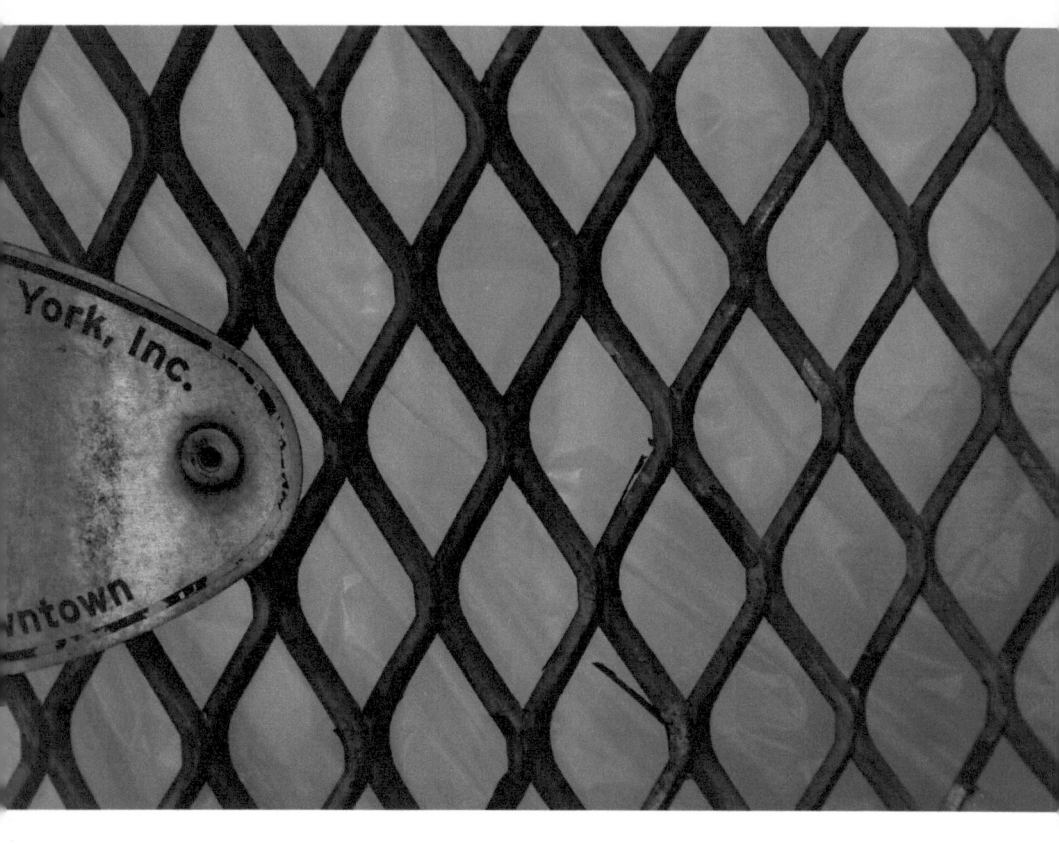

"We didn't think it would be this hard," said Jamil, speaking for several nodding passengers. "The bumps and curves on Mama Yah's road are making us miserable."

(Actually, it was the Two-Pound Giant Cotton Candy Surprise he had eaten that was making Jamil miserable, but he didn't say this. Perhaps he didn't even know it.)

Matt, who got no commission from Mama Yah's, had no real investment in going farther. But so far there had been no easy place to turn around. He started looking for one.

Andy and Ruby were so injured from fighting that they didn't want to go *anywhere.* If the bus had just stopped and dumped them out on the road in the middle of nowhere, they would have been happier.

Helen was so unhappy with how everyone on the bus had behaved that she also wanted off, just as long as it was somewhere different from Andy and Ruby.

Saura, who hadn't eaten yet, made a passionate plea that they had all started on a journey and they all should finish it. She thought the others would listen, but then Ryan talked about his experience at the restaurant that had used Mama Yah's Cookbook. He was *quite* sick and had little good to say about Mama Yah's recipes.

Just when it looked like the whole bus would vote to turn around, Jack spoke up. He was way in the back, and he couldn't easily be heard, but several people got his question up to Matt: Would they all be entitled to refunds if they didn't actually go to Mama Yah's Kitchen as promised?

When Matt finally heard the question, he blanched and quickly got on the microphone. "Thanks for all the comments," he said. "I understand that some of you may not feel like going into Mama Yah's Kitchen once we get there, and that's fine. You can stay on the bus and recuperate. But this *is* a tour to Mama Yah's Kitchen, and that's where we're going. And, by the way, there won't be any refunds. Thank you."

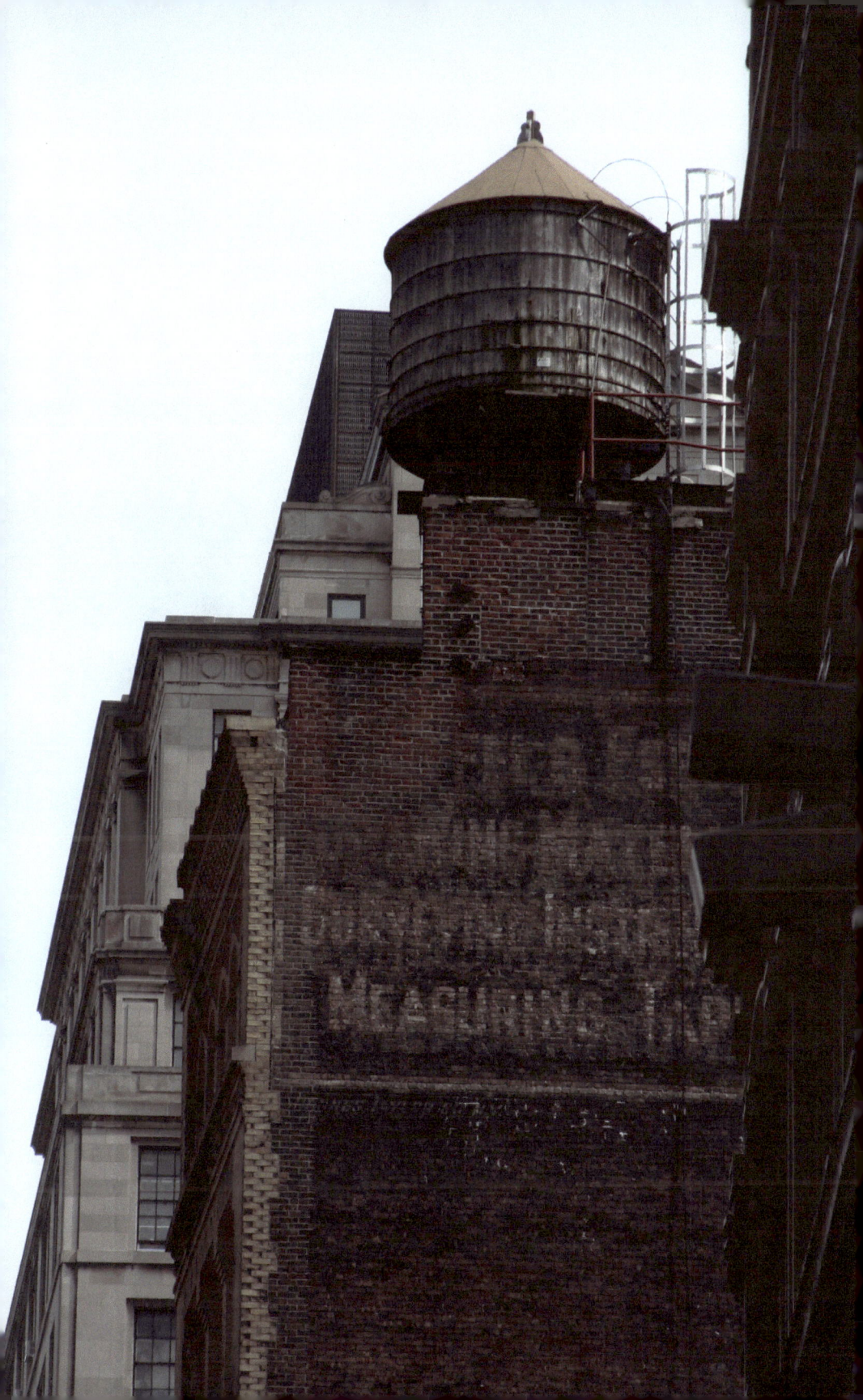

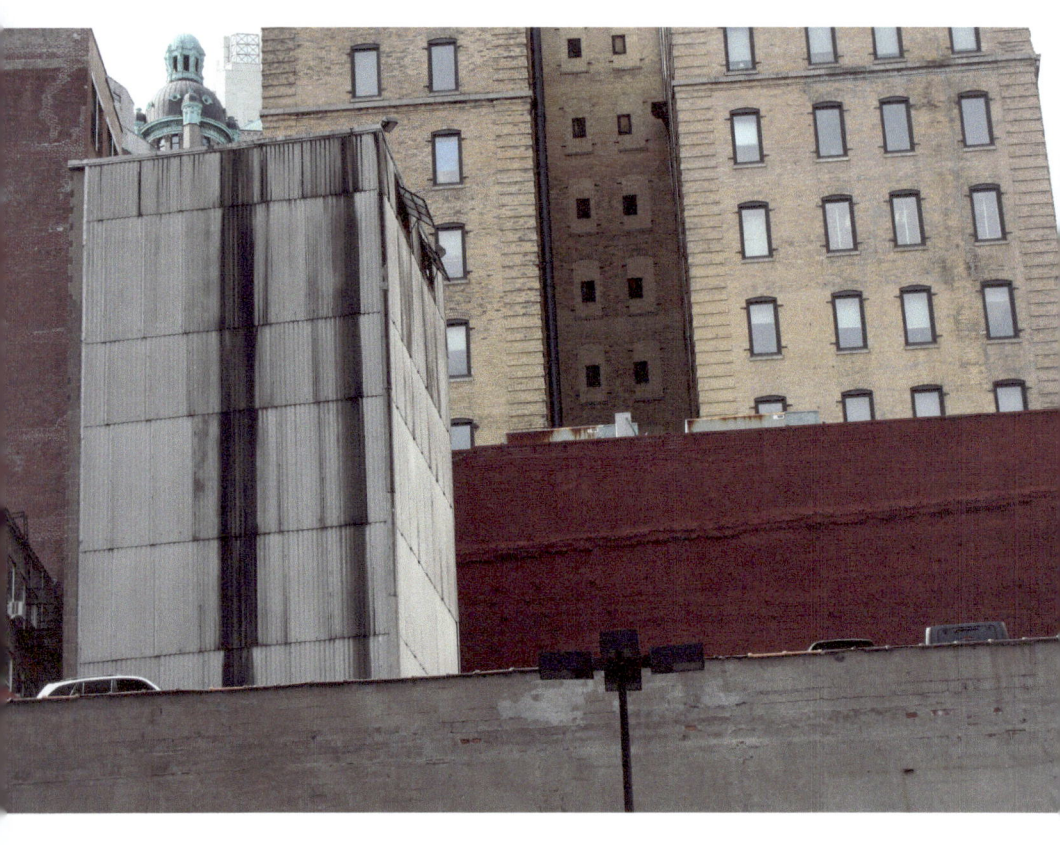

At this all the passengers quit talking and started looking out the windows, most having gotten quite a bit to think about over the last couple hours. The countryside was quite lovely. And then – much sooner than anyone expected – they arrived.

There were no flashing lights. There was no multi-colored neon arrow. There was no sign saying "EAT! EAT! EAT!" There was just a small, plainly printed notice that could be read when a person got up close to a rather plain building. "Everyone welcome here. Come in!"

Ryan and Floyd were too sick to leave the bus, and they nearly blocked everyone else. But Jamil forced his way through. Jamil still wasn't feeling well, but he liked to be out in front. Wen was right behind him. She still remembered the reputation of Mama Yah's mouth-watering deserts and fabulous entrees. Many other passengers eagerly followed.

Saura, however, was miserable.

Now that she was finally at Mama Yah's, she didn't want to go in. She'd been in a couple of the fights, and afterward she had peeked in a mirror. She was certain she was too unpresentable to go in, even though the sign clearly said everyone was welcome.

Saura stayed on board the bus and raised her eyebrows whenever anyone from a fight passed her. She silently convinced six people to remain on board. They all thought they probably wouldn't be accepted, even in a place as plain as Mama Yah's Kitchen appeared to be.

Andy decided to stay on the bus and finish his leftovers from the last stop.

Aki, who hadn't wanted to share his leftovers, decided he'd better stay on the bus to guard them so no one would steal them.

Helen decided to take *her* leftovers into Mama Yah's Kitchen and eat them there. She wanted to say she'd eaten at Mama Yah's Kitchen, but she didn't think she'd order anything more than what she already had.

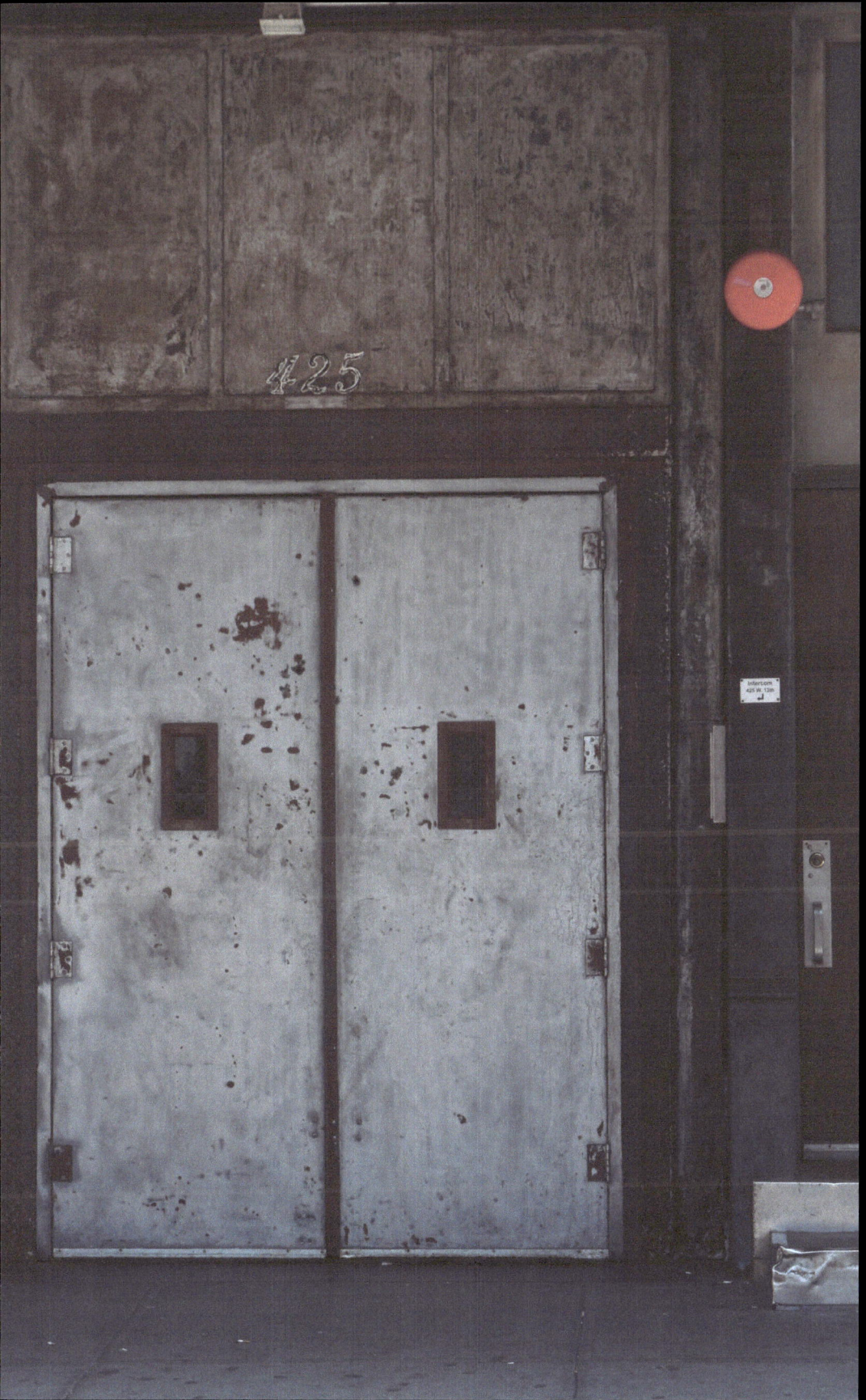

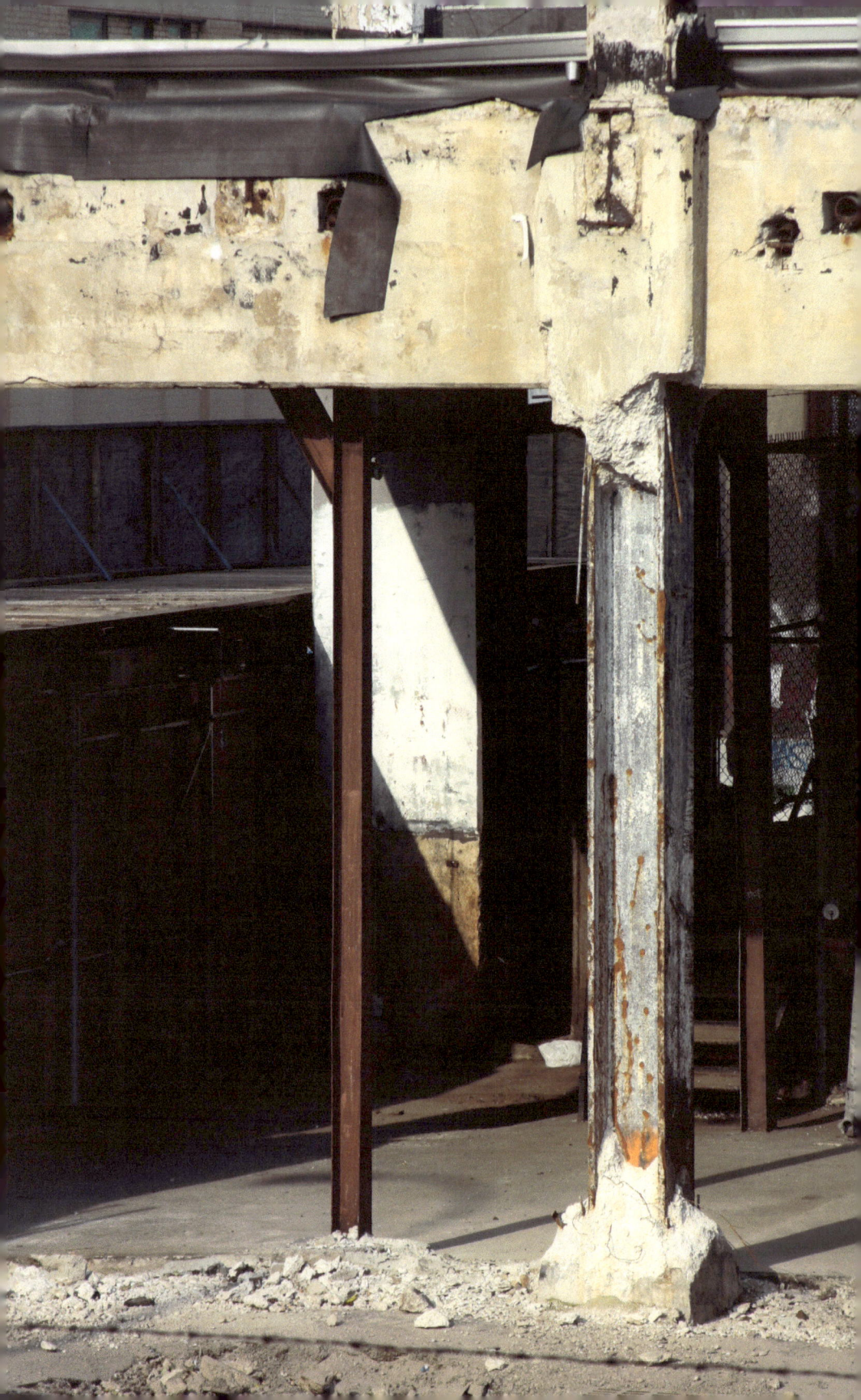

Isabel got off the bus because she wanted to find Mama Yah and tell her what she thought about her terrible recipe for Egg Custard Delight.

Between the people blocking others and the people hoarding and the people sick and the people trying to force their way off the bus, no one remembered Jack, who by now was quite hungry and quite sore from all the pushing and shoving. He was struggling to get to the front. He was quite slow and his way was frequently blocked by other passengers. A few new fights broke out as he struggled forward.

Jack had nearly made it to the front of the bus when Helen returned in a huff and pushed him back a few feet. She never did say what upset her so much, but she later admitted that she hadn't tried any of the food.

Then five more people stampeded back onto the bus, including Matt, all anxious to leave as soon as they could.

Matt jumped into the driver's seat, started the

bus, honked twice and began pulling out of the parking lot. Most of the passengers were already back on board (many had never left), and Matt didn't care about the rest. He knew from experience that anyone who stopped at Mama Yah's and actually tasted her food would want to stay.

The roar of the bus engine was so loud that Matt didn't hear Jack until he shifted gears. And then, in the small space of quiet between first and second, Matt heard Jack's small but clear voice. "Wait!"

Matt was in no mood to wait, and he almost pretended he didn't hear. But he realized that Jack was the one who had asked about the refund. Matt knew if he got Jack off the bus, he might have less trouble on the return trip. Matt planned to stop at the circle of restaurants again. He knew with Jack gone he might get away with a suggestion to the travelers that the great looking restaurants couldn't *all* be bad, and they should give them a second chance, visiting the ones they'd missed the first time. Matt was thinking about another commission. So he stopped the bus

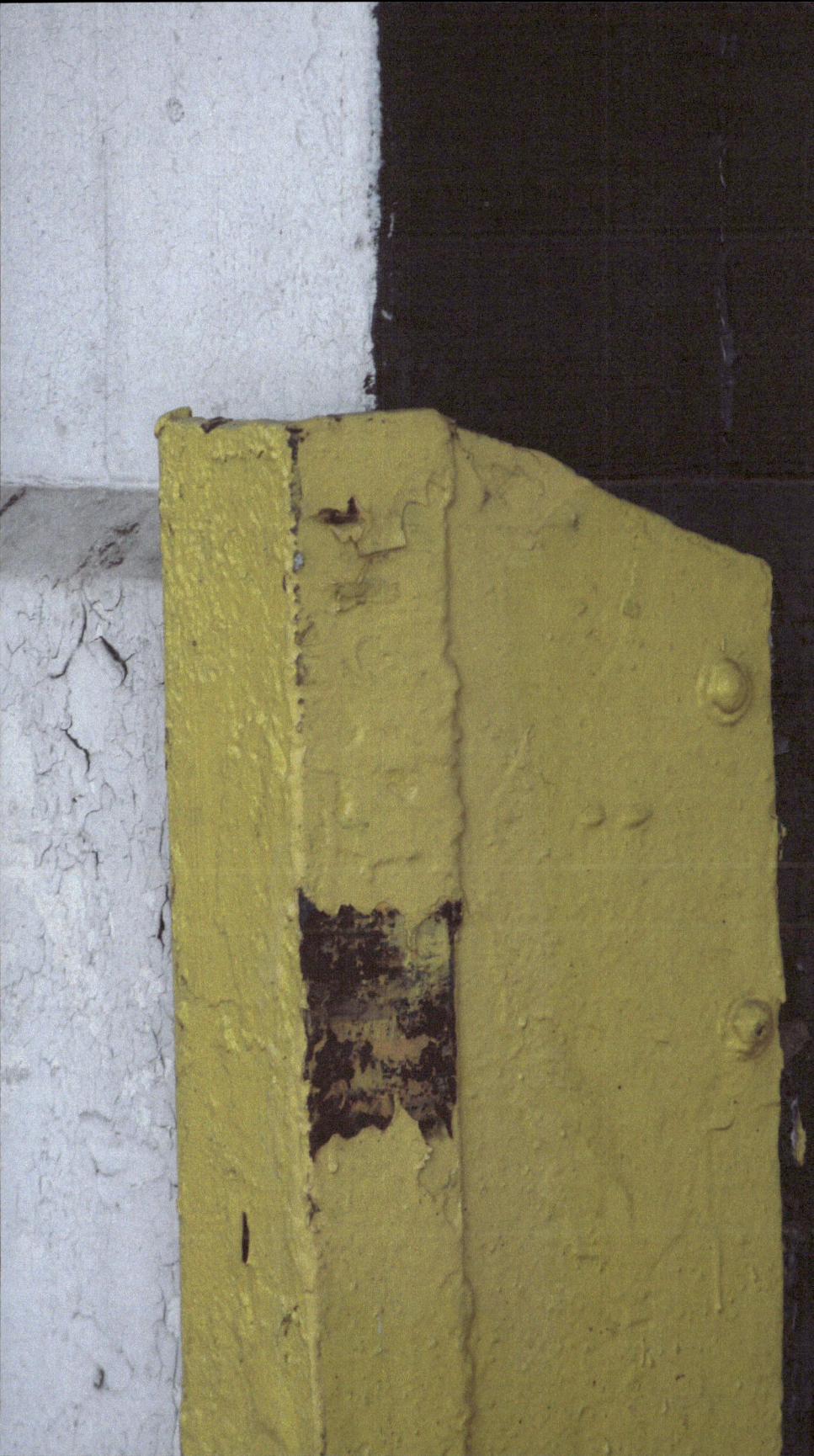

PARK

24
HRS.

Yoga to

to let Jack off. He left Jack a couple hundred yards outside the entrance to Mama Yah's enormous parking lot.

~

Inside Mama Yah's Kitchen, Javier, Ruby, Don, Wen, Caleb, Isabel and Jamil watched the bus pull away. Several of them had told Matt to go on without them. They had no desire to leave so soon, and they knew they could find another way back if they had to. And then – to their great surprise – Mama Yah *herself* came out of the kitchen and walked up to their table.

"I'm glad you're here," she said. "If you decide to stay, we could use your help around here. We can talk about that later. But first, aren't you forgetting something?"

They looked puzzled. Blank. No reaction.

"More specifically," Mama Yah said, "aren't you forgetting some *one*?"

They still looked puzzled. Lots of people had

stayed on the bus, but that was on purpose.

"Oh!" said Wen. "That boy who convinced the driver to finish the trip. He never made it into the restaurant!"

"That *is* too bad," said Jamil. "He'll miss this great dessert." Jamil was enjoying an Egg Custard Delight – a real one – which was far better than he had imagined. He didn't move.

But Wen was already out the door, into the parking lot. The first thing she saw was the bus, *far* in the distance, driving down the road.

That was too cruel, Wen thought, believing that Jack was still on board. Surely Mama Yah's timing could have been better. Just a minute earlier, and Wen could have caught the bus before it left.

Then Wen saw Jack, several feet from where he'd been dropped off, struggling to get to the restaurant. He wasn't making much progress, considering how far he had to go. His head was down, and he was slumped so much

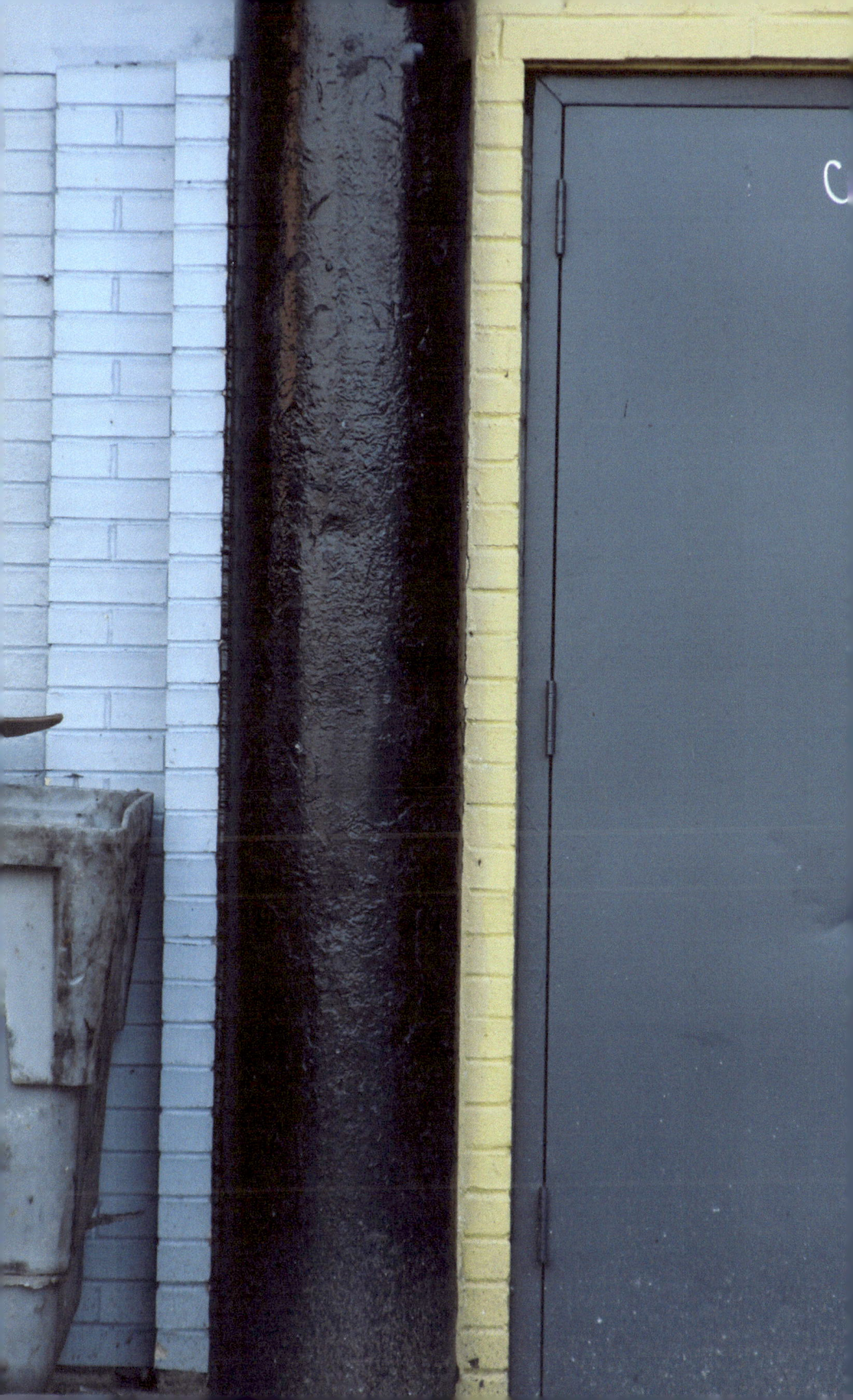

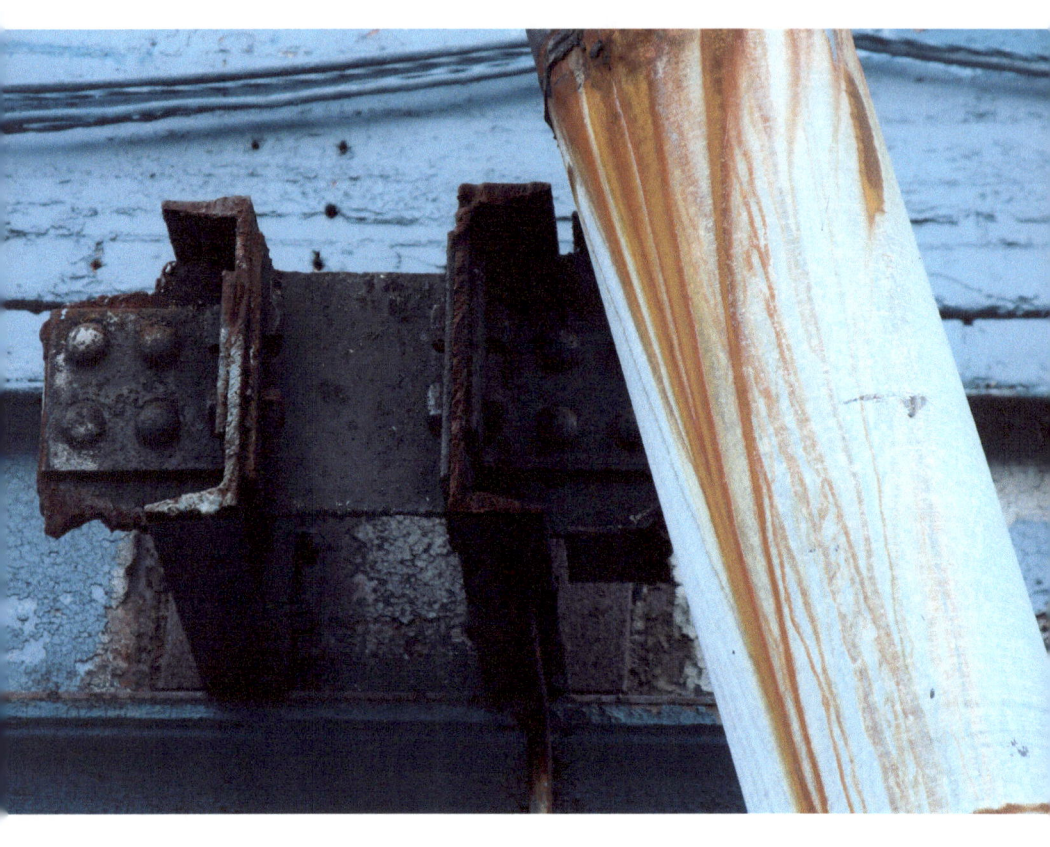

44

from dejection that Wen wasn't even sure at first that it *was* Jack. He'd given up hope. Jack didn't think he had the strength to make it to Mama Yah's even though he'd gotten so close.

Wen rushed towards him, her heart breaking at the sight.

She wasn't strong, but she was determined to be strong enough to get him to the restaurant. When she reached him, she introduced herself and – gently because of his bruises from the fights – began helping him struggle to the entrance. After a couple steps Wen wasn't sure she could do it. It was a long distance. But she was determined to try.

Then Jamil came out of the restaurant, finding that his Custard didn't taste quite as good when he knew he could help and didn't. He joined Wen, and they both helped Jack make his slow way to the entrance.

When the three arrived at the kitchen door, out came Mama Yah herself. She gave Jack a great big hug – a gentle one, owing to all his bruises, but a big one nonetheless.

Jack and Wen and Jamil and the others began helping Mama Yah run her restaurant that afternoon, and the more they ate her cooking, the more everyone wanted to stay.

Matt, meanwhile, made nearly as much money on his second stop at the circle of restaurants as he had at the first.

By the end of the trip, all the passengers on Matt's bus were so sick they told everyone they knew to avoid the trip to Mama Yah's. It was a *terrible* adventure, they said, and she was a *horrible* cook.

~ ~ ~

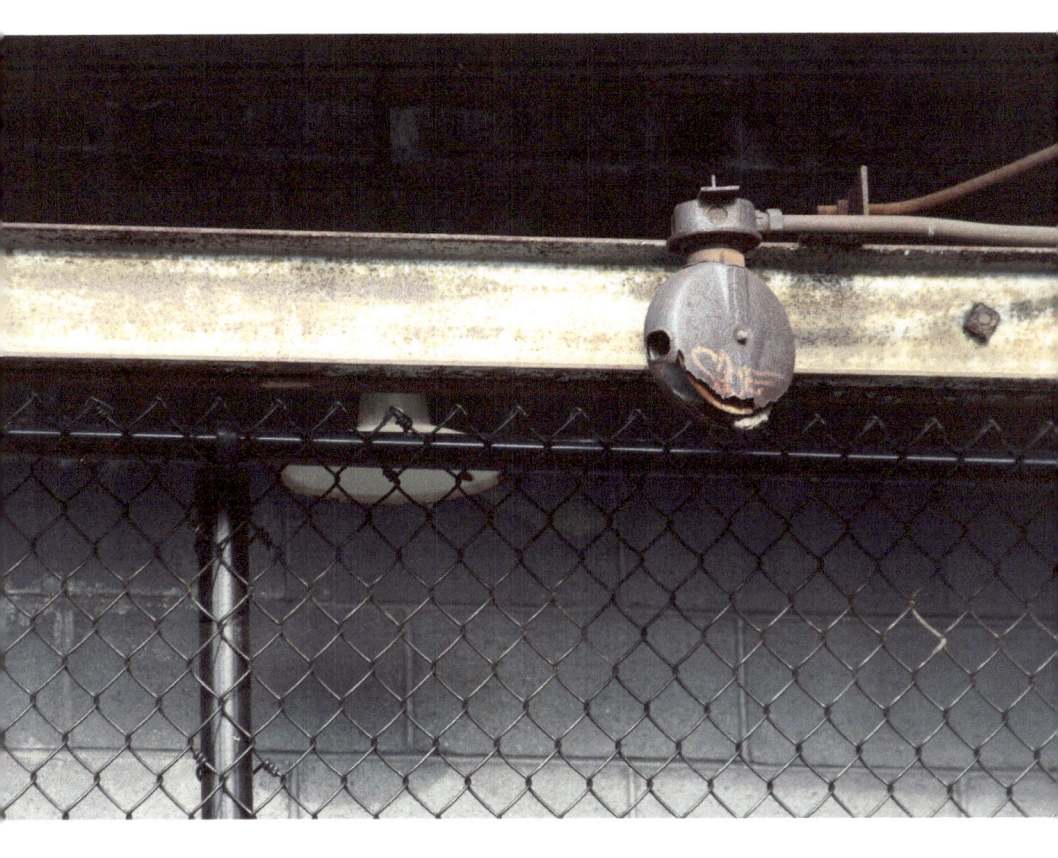

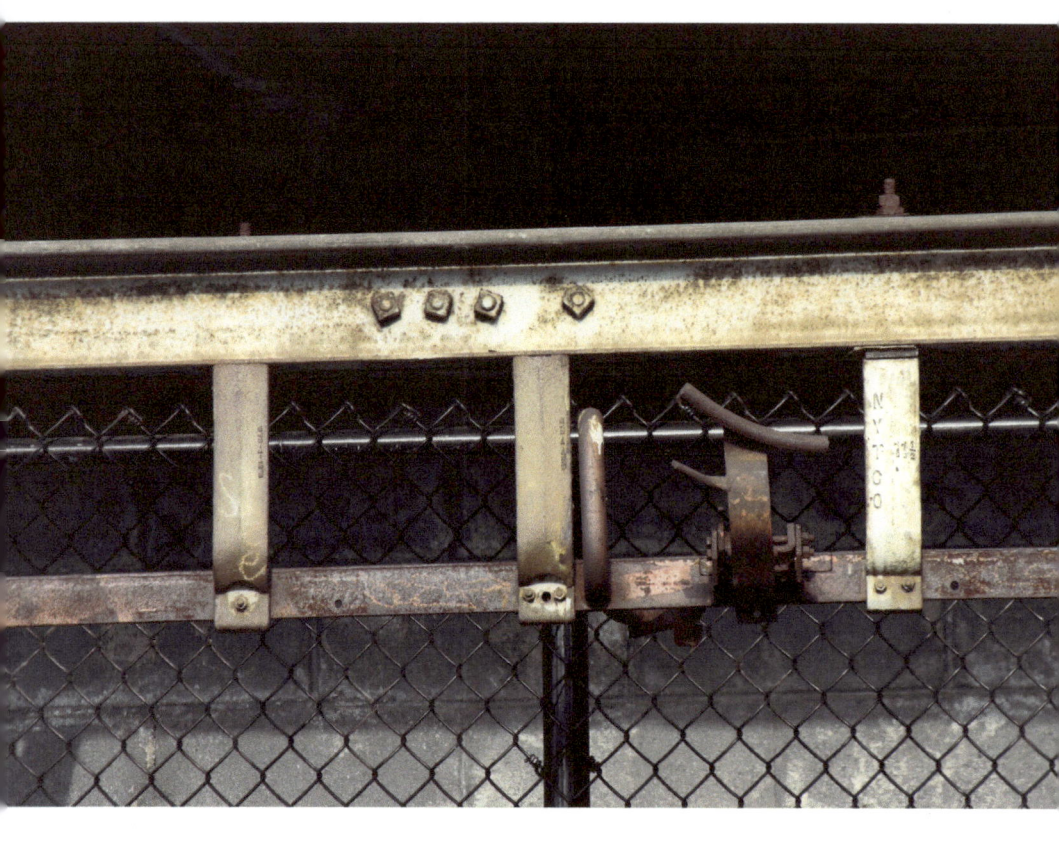

Reflection Questions

The passengers were headed to Mama Yah's Kitchen, but along the way they spoiled their appetites with some food that wasn't nearly as good.

What are the best and highest goals of *your* life?

What are some things you settle for instead?

Are you like any of the passengers on the bus?

How would you like to behave on the bus?

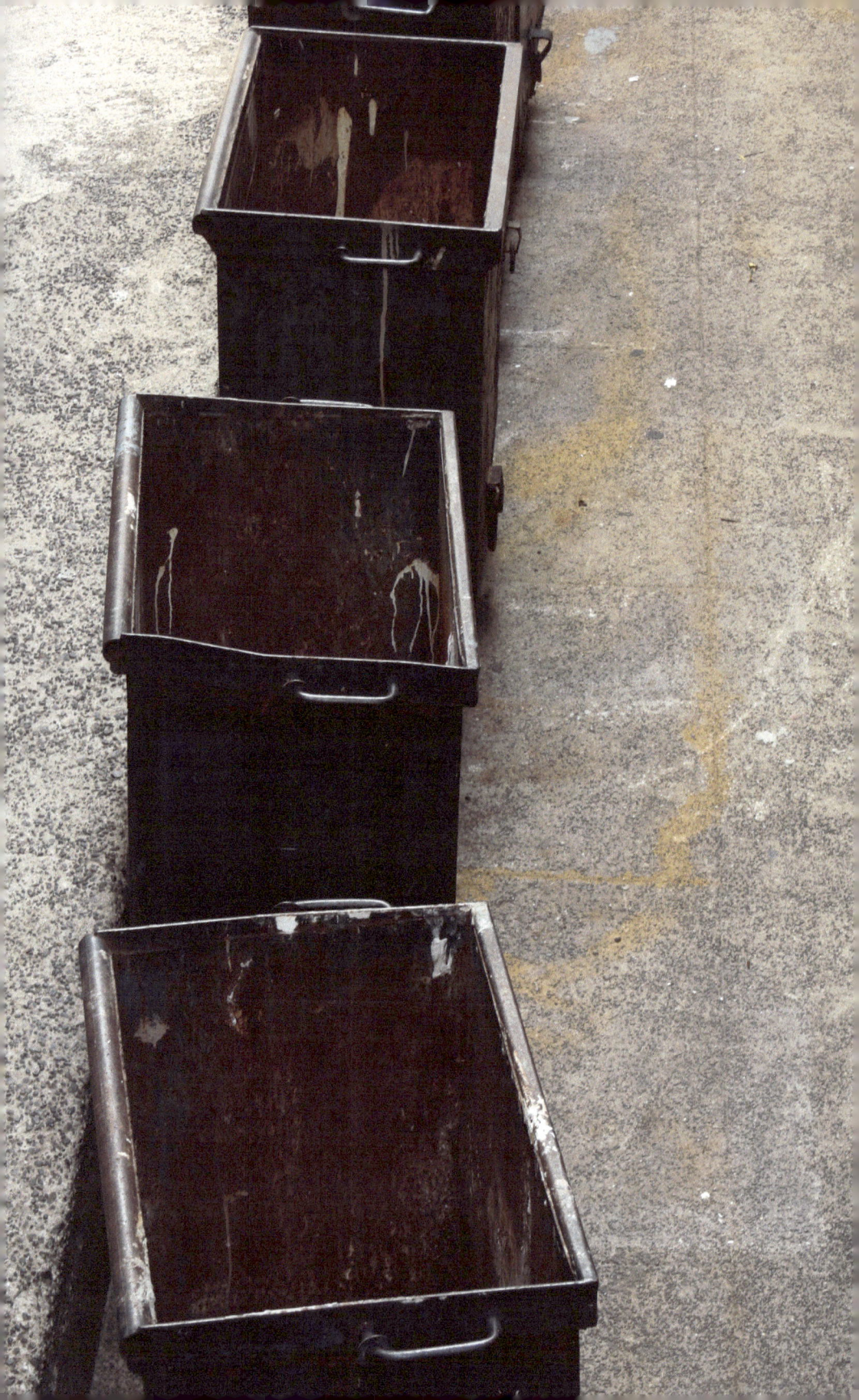

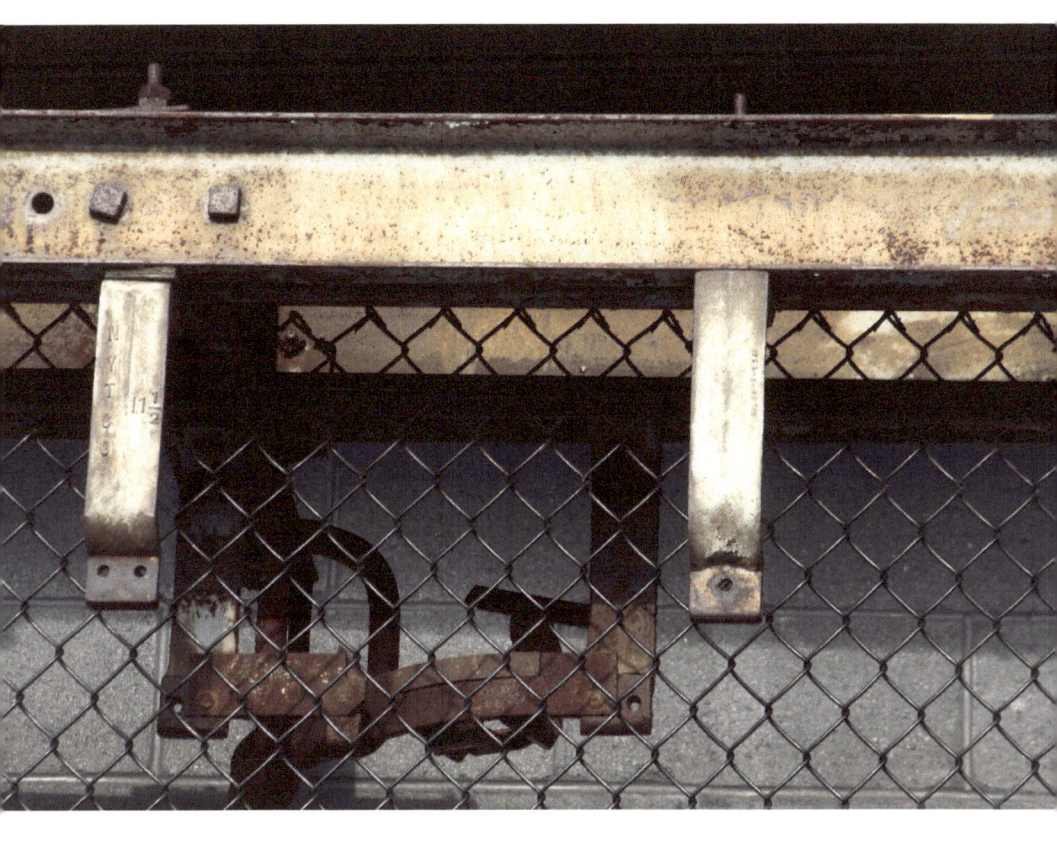

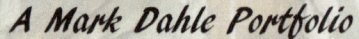

Amanda Gets A Pumpkin

(#1 in the series Amanda Wanted A Miracle)

This Mark Dahle Portfolio includes a colorful painting, twenty-four beautiful industrial photographs from Beijing, Shangahi and Xian, and a story about a girl who wanted a miracle.

"Oh dear," said her grandmother. "You didn't want a pumpkin? Perhaps we'll have to try again."

Teri's Renovation

This Mark Dahle Portfolio includes a painting, twenty-five beautiful industrial photos of New York, and a story about the renovation of Teri's house (which was a nightmare).

The contractor is an honest guy, so I'm certain he told Teri all the details, or at least some of them, at least in general. But maybe she wasn't listening.

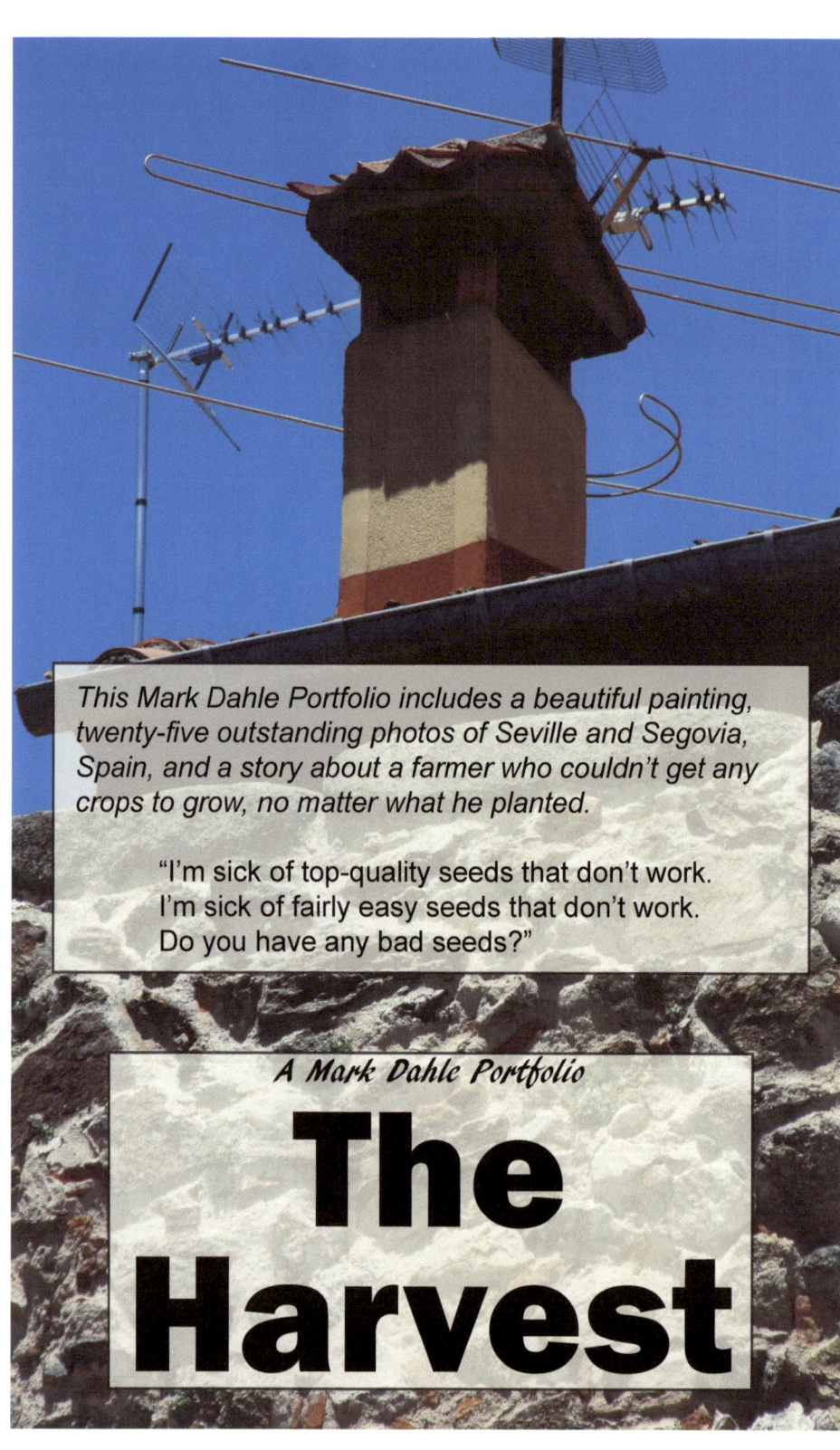

This Mark Dahle Portfolio includes a beautiful painting, twenty-five outstanding photos of Seville and Segovia, Spain, and a story about a farmer who couldn't get any crops to grow, no matter what he planted.

"I'm sick of top-quality seeds that don't work.
I'm sick of fairly easy seeds that don't work.
Do you have any bad seeds?"

A Mark Dahle Portfolio

The Harvest